FIGHTING THE GOOD FIGHT

* * * * *

Overcoming the Power of Your Enemy

* * * * *

PASTOR LARRY BRIGGS

ARGYLE FOX
PUBLISHING

Dedication

This is most likely one of my final and most important books and I, again, wholeheartedly dedicate it to my partner in ministry, my greatest encourager, and my best friend:

SARA JANE BRIGGS

I also dedicate this work to all the OVERCOMERS we have been privileged to pastor and minister to these past fifty-three years.

CONTENTS

PREFACE

He that hath an ear, let him hear what the Spirit saith unto the churches; to him that OVERCOMETH will I give to eat of the tree of life, which is in the midst of the paradise of God.—Revelation 2:7

He that hath an ear, let him hear what the Spirit saith unto the churches; He that OVERCOMETH shall not be hurt of the second death.—Revelation 2:11

He that hath an ear, let him hear what the Spirit saith unto the churches; To him that OVERCOMETH will I give to eat of the hidden manna, and will give him a white stone, and in the stone a new name written, which no man knoweth saving he that receiveth it.—Revelation 2:17

And he that OVERCOMETH and keepeth my works unto the end, to him will I give power over the nations.—Revelation 2:26

He that OVERCOMETH, the same shall be clothed in white raiment; and I will not blot out his name out of the book of life, but I will confess his name before my Father, and before his angels. He that hath an ear, let him hear what the Spirit saith unto the churches.—Revelation 3:5–6

Him that OVERCOMETH will I make a pillar in the temple of my God, and he shall go no more out: and I will write upon him the name of my God, and the name of the city of my God, which is new Jerusalem, which cometh down out of heaven from my God: and I will write upon him my new name. He that hath an ear, let him hear what the Spirit saith unto the churches.—Revelation 3:12–13

To him that OVERCOMETH will I grant to sit with me in my throne . . . He that hath an ear, let him hear what the Spirit saith to the churches.—Revelation 3:21–22

In 2015, I was stricken with a strange illness that resulted in my loss of memory and the ability to function on a daily basis. After two and one-half years of unspeakable pain and suffering, I was diagnosed with Lewy body dementia with Parkinson's disease and myoclonic seizures.

On May 5, 2017, the Director of the Psychological-Neurological Center at the University of Virginia Medical Center in Charlottesville, Virginia, told my wife, Jane, that I had two—maybe three—weeks to live. However, on Monday, July 31, 2017, I woke up totally healed with everything restored.

In the days to follow, the Holy Spirit began speaking personal and prophetic truths to my heart. He shared that I was not healed because I spent my entire life in ministry to others. Rather, I was healed because I am a child of God. The Spirit explained that the healing was for us—Jane and me, but the miracle was for the Church.

This insight led me to reread the book of Acts and to note every miracle, sign, and wonder performed by the early believers. As I obediently reread the book at the prompting of the

Spirit, He spoke a powerful word to my heart:

I want you to understand that when the Church was birthed, I used supernatural miracles of healing and signs and wonders to get peoples' attention so they would open their hearts to the Gospel and be saved. You are now living in the last days of the Church age, and I am going to end this dispensation the same way I started it—with a revival of the supernatural such as the Church has never seen in order to create a last-day revival that will result in the greatest harvest of souls the Church has ever experienced.

These past seven years, Jane and I have witnessed the beginning of this prophetic word. I believe that as the power and presence of God is manifested, we will also experience a rise in satanic activity. We see it today in every facet of culture and society. The root of the problems we're experiencing are not just political fallout, governmental chaos, or generational changes. They are the results of a nation turned from God, seeking to live in pleasure and decadence, with no acknowledgment of sin or wrong.

The crisis in crime is the direct result of a nation's rebellion against the fundamental Christian principles and teachings upon which we were built. Satan is at work, and we must prepare ourselves for the End-Time spiritual war prophesied throughout Scripture. We are literally living in the times Apostle Paul wrote about in Romans 1:21–25.

Because that, when they knew God, they glorified him not as God, neither were thankful; but became vain in their imaginations, and their foolish heart was darkened. Professing themselves to be wise, they became fools, and changed the glory of the incorruptible God into an image made like to corruptible man, and to birds, and four-footed beasts, and creeping things. Wherefore God also gave them up to uncleanness through the lusts of their own hearts, to dishonor their own bodies between themselves: who changed the truth of god into a lie, and worshiped and served the creature more than the creator, who is blessed forever. Amen.

We are in a daily war but the good news (Gospel) is that the battle has already been won by Jesus Christ, our Lord and Savior, who died for us on the cross at Calvary. According to Peter, Christ has given us everything we need to be overcomers. "According to His divine power hath given unto us all things that pertain unto life and godliness, through the knowledge of Him that hath called us to glory and virtue" (2 Peter 2:3)

The Apostle John proclaims the same truth as he records in the revelation given to him on the Island of Patmos. "And they overcame him by the blood of the lamb, and by the word of their testimony; and they loved not their lives unto the death." (Revelation 12:11)

As we begin this study, let's do so understanding that we are already **overcomers**. Our responsibility is to live in the victory Jesus has provided for us by living a life of faith and obedience that will bring glory and honor to Him who loved us and gave Himself as a sacrifice for our sins.

INTRODUCTION

The first three chapters of the book of Revelation intro-
duce us to the idea that God expects us to be overcomers. As stated in the previous printed verses, He has
reserved special blessings to those who live faithful and fruitful
lives for His glory.

From its birth in the book of Acts until now, the Church
has been under attack. In Matthew 11:12, Jesus spoke of this
spiritual war: "And from the days of John the Baptist until now
the Kingdom of Heaven suffers violence, and the violent take
it by force." You and I are privileged to live in one of the most
strategic times of God's eternal plan for all ages. Every believer
in Jesus Christ has been born with purpose and a planned destiny. If we are going to discover and fulfill that destiny, we must
be overcomers.

Each one of us must cultivate an intimate and personal relationship with Jesus on a daily basis. It is through our relationship with Him that we live as victors not victims. The Apostle
Paul wrote concerning our battles:

*Nay, in all these things we are more than conquerors
through Him that loved us. For I am persuaded, that neither
death, nor life, nor angels, nor principalities, nor powers, nor*

things present, nor things to come, nor height, nor depth, nor any other creature, shall be able to separate us from the love of God, which is in Christ Jesus." (Romans 8:37–39)

In submitting ourselves to the lordship of Christ in every area of our lives, we can abort Satan's attempts to conquer us, weaken the Church, and render Christ's Church powerless and ineffective.

Jesus did not give birth to a weak, cowardly Church. He birthed a bold and aggressive body of believers who would bravely trample into Satan's territory, knowing that the gates of Hell could not withstand their power and authority. As disciples of Jesus Christ, we are empowered by the Holy Spirit to confront and conquer our enemy, who is identified by Paul in Ephesians 6:12: "For we do not wrestle against flesh and blood but against principalities, against powers, against the rulers of darkness of this age, against spiritual hosts of wickedness in heavenly places."

From creation until now, this spiritual war has been in process. The battle is between God and Satan (Lucifer), the fallen archangel and his cohorts. In John 10:10, Jesus clearly defines Satan's mission. "The thief does not come except to steal, and to kill, and to destroy. . . . I have come that they may have life, and that they may have it more abundantly." In his epistles to the early Church, the Apostle Peter writes concerning this same battle. In 1 Peter 5:8, he writes, "Be sober, be vigilant; because your adversary the devil walks about like a roaring lion, seeking whom he may devour."

The battle lines have clearly been drawn. In order to win this war, we must stay prepared and keep our focus on Jesus, the author and finisher of our faith. (Hebrews 12:2) The closer we get to the end of time, the more intense the battles will become. But we should not live in fear. Rather, we must live by faith in the Son of God, who has already won the war for us. Our role is to cultivate a personal relationship with Him and walk in the Spirit so we will be aware of the enemy's schemes and not be fooled or distracted by him, "Lest Satan should get an advantage of us: for we are not ignorant of his devices." (2 Corinthians 2:11)

Some of the greatest battles we face are in our minds. Satan knows our weaknesses and where we are most vulnerable. As we embark on this study together, it is my prayer that you be equipped with fresh knowledge from God's Word and a practical understanding of how to use it to defeat your enemies. Remember, **we have been made more than conquerors.** (Romans 8) If we are willing to keep an open heart and a teachable spirit, the Holy Spirit will guide us into truth that will set us free, and whom the Son sets free is free indeed!

MEDITATION 1
PREPARING FOR BATTLE

"The Spirit of the Lord is upon me, because He has anointed me to preach the Gospel to the poor; He has sent me to heal the brokenhearted, to proclaim liberty to the captives and recovery of sight to the blind, to set at liberty those who are oppressed; to proclaim the acceptable year of the Lord."—Luke 4:15,18,19, 21

These words spoken by the Prophet Isaiah some 700 years before the birth of Jesus was a divine mission statement for Jesus's ministry and the Church He would birth. Jesus came to heal all who were oppressed. He brought spiritual, emotional, and physical healing to a wounded world. As you begin this study, I encourage you to pause briefly and take a serious look at your life.

Many of God's people are struggling with defeat in their walk with Him because of past hurts and disappointments. If ignored, these bruises develop into spiritual cancers that can hinder or even destroy us. Satan will use everything possible to keep us from the life of victory that Jesus purchased for us.

In order to be healed, we must identify what issues hold us back. Once we acknowledge them, we can bring them to the cross for healing and deliverance. This is a major step in becoming the overcomer He desires us to be.

It is not an easy battle, but it can be won. We are weakened by our woundedness, and we must first seek healing in order to remain strong in the daily battles that we must fight. We must allow the Holy Spirit to illuminate specific scriptures, such as Romans 8:39 and Philippians 4:13, which wield the power to comfort and heal whatever bruises you are nursing. God knows exactly where you are on your journey and what you need. Trust Him to lead you as you prepare for future battles. "God is our refuge and strength, a very present help in trouble." (Psalm 46:1)

After bringing our bruises and wounds to the cross for healing, we must begin careful preparation and strategic planning. In his writing to the Galatians, the Apostle Paul taught the importance of walking in the Spirit. "This I say then, walk in the Spirit, and ye shall not fulfill the lust of the flesh." (Galatians 5:16) Walking denotes a lifestyle, not a one-time event. You can't get into physical shape with a single visit to the gym. You must daily cultivate an intimate relationship with Jesus through the indwelling of His Holy Spirit.

This is a journey in which we renounce the things of this world and all of our fleshly appetites on a daily basis. Our hunger and thirst must be for God and His righteousness. "But seek ye first the Kingdom of God, and His righteousness; and all these things will be added unto you." (Matthew 6:33)

Jesus warned us about falling in love with the things of this world. We are also exhorted in Hebrews to rid ourselves of anything that hinders us from living in victory. "Wherefore seeing we also are compassed about with so great a cloud of witnesses, let us lay aside every weight, and the sin which doth so easily beset us, and let us run with patience the race that is set before us." (Hebrews 12:1)

Walking in the Spirit ensures victory, but it must be done intentionally with purposeful planning and consistent preparation. There are several areas in life we must focus on in order to stay prepared for victory.

1. FOCUS

We must be willing and able to fix our focus. The things we focus on direct our thinking and actions. There are many scriptural examples of this principle. One of my favorites is the story of David conquering Goliath.

David found his brothers hiding in fear, because all they saw was how large the enemy was. In contrast, David kept his eyes on God. As a result, he was able to win the battle.

We all face giants on our journey. If we focus on the problem, we will end up in defeat. However, if we follow David's example and keep our focus on the problem-solver—Jesus—and allow the Holy Spirit to fix our focus, we will see and understand how big our God is. This will increase our faith and confidence in battle, knowing He is with us and bringing us into victory.

This is accomplished through discipline and saturating our hearts and minds with the Word of God.

Remember: Our God is a miracle-working God who has already won the battle for us. As we keep our eyes on Him, we will see and understand that there is no devil, disease, problem, or relationship He can't conqueror for us.

2. LIFESTYLE

An equally important area pertaining to our walk focuses on our lifestyle.

This may sound elementary, but how we live on a daily basis ultimately determines our destination. We must embrace a Christian worldview and commit ourselves to living by the principles taught in the Word of God. Society is ever-changing, but God's Word is forever set.

We ought not be tossed about by our changing culture as those who have no anchor. We are not of this world, and our convictions and practices are not determined by what people think or accept.

We currently live in a world that is morally confused, literally not knowing right from wrong. We cannot follow those standards and live in victory. We must cultivate a lifestyle based solely on God's Word, specifically the principles taught in the Ten Commandments. These laws were originally given to show our need for Jesus. They were never intended to be restrictive or legalistic, but rather to reveal the character of our Heavenly Father, serving as a compass for living successfully in a broken and confused world.

In His Sermon on the Mount, Jesus brought these truths to life. He emphasized that living by them would guarantee blessings.

We are not here simply to live and experience happiness and pleasure. Our divine purpose is to reflect Jesus Christ to a dark and lost world. We can only do this by living as He lived on this earth. It requires much prayer, discipline, and intentional living. Many of us need to make serious changes in our lifestyles. This can only be done through the power of the Holy Spirit dwelling in us.

3. DESIRE

As we continue to seek a life walking in the Spirit that results in our being overcomers, we must address our desires.

Our personal desires motivate us in every area of our lives. In order for positive change to occur in our lives, there must first be a genuine desire to change.

In my fifty-three years of pastoral ministry, I have encountered many believers who were sincerely sick and tired of losing and being victimized in their daily walks. They expressed a deep hatred for the life they lived. They felt their lives were caused by a heavy burden of self-justified anger aimed at people and circumstances that contributed to their failures. These bitter believers walked around with the needless baggage of resentfulness, blindly believing things will never change.

Does this sound familiar? Such people are greatly hindered in breaking free from their attitude because they adopted a victim mentality. They are quick to judge others, and they make no apology for blaming their problems on everyone and everything. The truth is that no person, government, agency, nor circumstance can imprison and defeat you unless you allow it.

Life is not always fair, even for us who believe in and are committed to living for Jesus. Our attitude in and reaction to these situations determines the outcome. When I acknowledge that my actions are birthed in my attitude about life, then I can focus on the real issue and take control by allowing the Holy Spirit to change my desires. I must cultivate right thinking, and this begins with a sincere desire to change. This desire is not to change my circumstances. It is to change me—or rather, to recognize and live out the change Christ states is already mine.

People usually get what they desire. This is especially true in our microwave generation, which is built on instant gratification regardless of the cost. If we really want something, regardless of how difficult it may be to obtain and the consequences we must pay to have it, we will find a way to get it.

The stubbornness and strength of the human spirit is both a liability and an asset. The drug addict will always find a way to get his or her fix. The alcoholic will always find a way to the bottle. The nicotine addict will always justify smoking regardless of all the health warnings. The food addict will easily find the way back to the buffet bar three or four times. The sex addict will always find excuses and be convinced such a lifestyle is normal and such actions are okay. The power-hungry executive will always find a way to the top in spite of those he or she must hurt to get there.

In psychology, therapists work with a principle that states, "Until the pain of an individual's destructive habits outweigh the gain, change will never happen." Unfortunately, this has proven true even in the lives of believers in Jesus Christ. We allow our feelings to overrule our faith, and we live as victims rather than as overcomers.

To experience healing, we must confront our wrong thinking, come to the cross, and like David, ask God to search our hearts and create within us a right spirit (desire). Jesus taught that true happiness comes to those who hunger for and seek righteousness. What you focus on, you hunger for and passionately seek to acquire. With personal desires, we must be totally honest with ourselves and most importantly, with God. If your greatest desires are focused on the flesh and the things of this world, admit it. Then repent and allow the Holy Spirit to daily renew your mind.

That you put off concerning the former conversation the old man, which is corrupt according to the deceitful lusts; and be renewed in the spirit of your mind. And that you put on the new man, which after God is created in righteousness and true holiness. (Ephesians 4:22–24)

Pray specifically that He will create in you a sincere desire to change, then cultivate that desire through prayer and meditation on God's Word. It will greatly help to maintain this desire if you get involved in a local Spirit-filled church that can foster your spiritual growth. This is one of the main reasons we are exhorted in Hebrews 10:25: "not forsaking the assembling of ourselves together, as the manner of some is; but exhorting one another: and so much the more, as you see the day approaching."

As the End Times quickly approach, we need each other and the Church more than ever. We draw strength from the fellowship and teaching of our faith community. By renouncing sinful habits and wrong thinking and staying close to the Cross, your desires will change and you will feel differently.

Desire is a strong motivator. If we daily cultivate pure desires before God, it will create a constant hunger for righteousness.

4. DECISIONS

As significant a role as desire plays, changing desires alone will not sustain victory in all our battles. The next critical issue we must give careful attention to is our personal decision-making process.

We are all creatures of habit. Regardless of how strong our desire for change may be, too often we revert back to the same old habits and lifestyles. In doing so, we become more addicted than before.

I am a strong believer in the saving grace of God, but I also believe in and understand the power of free will. God will not force us to live for Him. He has done everything to open the door to following Him, but the choice is up to us. Therefore, desire must be reinforced by decision.

We must intentionally make good choices to change our way of thinking. As we do this, we change how we live. Learning how to make good decisions is the focus of our next chapter, but here I will stress the importance of preparation by drawing our focus on this important issue.

Desire always produces a decision, whether good or bad. To sustain good decisions we must develop discipline in our lives. As we discuss in the next chapter, most of us make decisions based on feelings. That's why we must see the connection between desire and decision.

In every situation in life, we are presented with a decision. For Christians, the best decisions are based on faith, not feelings. Basing decisions on faith requires self-control and discipline.

We are born again by the grace of God, but that does not change the responsibility brought about by free will. God gives us the privilege and responsibility to choose daily how we will live. Every day I am confronted with decisions that will affect my relationship with God, my family, and others. If you aim to live free from destructive habits that Satan uses to destroy you, you must make a decision to be free. One fruit of the Spirit is self-control. Walk in Him, and He will enable you to develop discipline and self-control in your life.

Once you decide to follow Jesus, you must address the issue

of discipline in your life. The very word discipline makes us uncomfortable, especially in today's culture. We are programmed to believe that we're entitled to everything we want, and we deserve to have it all now. We desperately need to examine this unbiblical concept and embrace the principles and values that govern the Kingdom of God. Remember, we are not of this world. So, we must personally take to heart Jesus's teachings that we are to live separate from and not love the things of this world. Only God, through the indwelling power of the Holy Spirit, can help us win this battle.

Jesus's teachings were not only rejected by the hierarchy of His day, but also led to His crucifixion. It is no different today. We may be more sophisticated in our lifestyles, enjoying personal pleasures made easy by technology, but the end result is the same. As Scripture teaches, if we sow according to the flesh, we will reap what the flesh produces. If we live according to the Spirit, we will receive from the Spirit fruit that results in abundance in every area of our lives.

As previously stated, self-control is a fruit of the Spirit. Paul taught in the book of Romans that the battle between the flesh and the Spirit never ceases. He also emphatically stated that we can win this war by submitting to the lordship of Jesus Christ through the power of the Holy Spirit. Out of a pure desire, we can be motivated to make right decisions. But without discipline, we fail. In Romans chapters eight through twelve, Paul teaches the three steps to a disciplined life: submission, surrender, and sacrifice.

5. DETERMINATION

Another principle required in maintaining a victorious life is developing an attitude of determination. I can't say that one step is more important than the others, but determination is critical.

On this journey with Christ, all of us slip and fall—including me. Including you. You will encounter obstacles and make mistakes. When you do, remind yourself that Jesus is a friend who sticks closer than a brother and will never leave you. He is a present help in times of trouble (Psalms 46), and He is there to pick you up. Remembering this in difficult times is critical.

Whatever you do, don't give up. God has destined you for a specific pathway. He will empower you by His Spirit to finish the race. Don't become distracted by disappointment and discouragement. Rather, through prayer and the Word, develop a strong mindset of determination.

When you do fall, consider what direction you were headed. Were you walking toward the cross or away from it? If you train yourself to always keep the cross in your focus, you will become the person you want to be, the person He has designed you to become.

Determination will always help you keep going. It will assist you in navigating the rough places successfully. Remember, determination is a battle of the mind and can only be won as we allow the Holy Spirit to daily renew our thinking processes.

You will get tired and grow weary—both physically and spiritually—and there will be plenty of opportunities to quit. But determination, partnered with the power of the Holy Spirit working in you, will keep you focused and moving forward.

In summary, if you cultivate a pure desire and prayerfully make the right decisions, sustained by self-discipline reinforced by an unshakable determination, you will always be a victor not a victim, enjoying the benefits of overcomers!

MEDITATION 2

OVERCOMING BAD DECISIONS

Multitudes, multitudes in the valley of decision: for the day of the Lord is near in the valley of decision.—Joel 3:14

And if it seem evil unto you to serve the Lord, choose you this day whom ye will serve; whether the gods which your Fathers served that were on the other side of the flood, or the gods of the Amorites, in whose land you dwell: but as for me and my house, we will serve the Lord. —Joshua 24:15

I noted in the previous chapter that developing a good decision-making process is one of five values we must focus on to live a victorious life. Because this is so critical, I want to note some practical thoughts on this issue.

The prophet Joel refers to the valley of decision, a place each of us will find ourselves in from time to time. Learning to make good decisions is one of the most important life skills that we can acquire. Unfortunately, many assume we will develop this skill as we age and grow in experience.

I have nearly eighteen years of formal education including college and graduate level studies, yet I have never been offered a course in decision-making. That's because we assume it is something we learn by trial and error. The reality is that decisions have consequences, here and now. Every decision I make impacts my relationship with God, my family, and others. Your destiny and the quality of your life are determined by your personal decision-making process. Our Heavenly Father has a plan and purpose for each of our lives, but He leaves it up to us to decide how we will live. The biblical truth is that your destiny is in your hands and ultimately will be determined by the daily decisions you make.

Because this is so important, I encourage you to pause your reading and prayerfully evaluate how you make decisions. You may not have your decision-making process written down or outlined, but you use a process to make decisions. If you review your life with absolute honesty, you will see that you are where you are and who you are because of past decisions.

Each of us develops a personal belief system as we grow into adulthood. Out of those beliefs, we make decisions. The principles or values by which we live are birthed within that system. This is why it is so critical that we choose a lifestyle patterned after the Word of God and that we commit to live in accord with God's Word.

Our personal convictions ought not be determined by our culture but by our faith. In America, we have abandoned the biblical principles upon which this great nation was built. In so doing, we have lost our moral compass. Many believers have been caught up in this lie. They've developed a belief system based on the thinking of our so-called free society in which everything is permissible and entitlement and self-gratification are the norm. The sad results are that many brothers and sisters in faith make decisions based on what culture accepts and allows rather than on what the Bible teaches.

Cultures change constantly, but God's Word never does. If it was sin in the Bible, it is still sin today, regardless of how popular it is. Every decision we make is based on the personal principles we live by, and every decision has a consequence, whether good or bad. That is why it is imperative to allow the Holy Spirit to search our hearts as we prayerfully consider how we make decisions. Periodically, we must examine our belief system to ensure it is based on God's Word and not the worldly culture.

If you take a sincere look at some of the major decisions you made in life, you may discover that—like most of us—you made those decisions based on how you felt in the moment. Sometimes, our feelings are correct. But in many situations, you can't trust them. Emotions can cloud the truth and result in bad decisions. This is why we are exhorted in Proverbs: "Trust in the Lord with all thine heart; and lean not unto thine own understanding. In [all] thy ways acknowledge Him, and He shall direct thy ways." (Proverbs 3:5–6)

Because our physical senses are so strong, we are often influenced by them rather than by faith or fact. Poor decisions are made when we are guided by wrong principles. Good decisions are always the result when we are directed by the Holy Spirit and the principles taught in the Word of God.

Discipline and self-control are major components of the decision-making process. Through discipline and self-control you can train yourself to respond rather than react in any situation.

A response is made through reasoning, knowledge, and facts. A reaction is based on feelings. We must learn to think before we act.

A response produces positive results, while a reaction often produces negative results. Learning to respond (think) before you react (act) is an acquired skill that takes practice and effort. It may never be automatic or spontaneous, but it can be achieved through the power of the Holy Spirit and discipline. As believers, we must learn to walk in the Spirit, not our feelings. Please understand that I am not suggesting you ignore your feelings. Our Heavenly Father created us as physical, spiritual, and emotional beings. Our feelings are important, but we must allow our faith to lead us, not our feelings. Learning this will help us achieve positive results.

Over the years, I have developed a decision-making process as a husband, father, and pastor. It is not foolproof, but it works well for me. If you find it helpful, you can use it as a blueprint to develop your own. That said, please understand this is a very personal matter. What works for one person may not work for all. Individualize your plan to suit your personality and temperament. Developing and writing down a personal plan will aid you in making good decisions by putting everything into perspective.

My plan involves seven carefully planned steps.

1. Gain information and seek to see the big picture.
2. Identify all problems associated with the situation.
3. Consider the current circumstances.
4. Explore all possible options.
5. Make a prayerful decision.
6. Develop a practical plan to reach the conclusion.
7. Evaluate the plan and process.

Before closing this chapter, I need to discuss an uncomfortable but necessary question. How do we deal with and survive poor decisions of the past? All of us have made bad decisions. Even now, you may be living with the regret and unfavorable consequences of bad decisions you made in the past. I, too, have suffered from bad decisions, and I know how hard they can make life.

Thankfully, our bad decisions don't have the last word. We serve a loving God who can turn our messes into great messages. Romans 8:28 has become one of my anchor scriptures that I look to very often: "And we know that all things work together for good to them that love God, to them who are called according to His purpose."

If you are currently living with the consequences of bad decisions, be encouraged. You can overcome this and get back on the right path where you want to be, where God has destined you to be.

Let me suggest four simple but difficult steps that will help get you there.

1. FACE IT

You have to be honest and big enough to admit your mistakes. Stop the blame game and take ownership of your life. Break the cycle by confessing your wrong, sincerely repenting and prayerfully asking your Heavenly Father to help you. He will.

2. FIX IT

Once you have faced it, prayerfully seek ways to fix it. Sometimes the damage may be irreparable, but seek forgiveness from God. Then seek forgiveness from those who were hurt by your actions.

Do whatever you can to make it right. If you lied, correct it by telling the truth; if you stole, work out a repayment plan.

If you have offended someone, apologize in person if possible. Whatever you have done, if you pray and seek the wisdom of your Heavenly Father through the Holy Spirit, He will show you how to correct it if it can. If it can't be corrected, humble yourself before God and ask Him to give you the strength to take the next step.

3. FORGET IT

Step three is easier to say than do. If you can't fix it, then by the power of the Holy Spirit, commit it to God and forget it. That's right, just forget it and move forward, having learned from your mistake.

I know some people will not let you forget it, and the devil will often use those people to remind you of your past sin. Get in God's Word and allow the Holy Spirit to illuminate your heart and mind. People may refuse to forget, but God doesn't work that way.

In Psalm 103, the psalmist tells us that God has taken all our sins and cast them into a sea never to remember them again. Your Heavenly Father doesn't focus on your past, so why should you? It's not where you've been that matters. It's where you're going. Fix your focus on Jesus and the cross and keep moving forward. In Him alone you can experience complete forgiveness and a new start. When you fully embrace and understand this truth, you are ready to take the final step.

4. FOCUS ON THE FUTURE

Don't let your past destroy your future. God will help you recover and restore everything the enemy has taken.

Get involved in a good, local Bible-believing church and learn to live in God's amazing grace that flows out of His unconditional love for you. Cultivate close friendships with other believers and be a contributing member of your faith community.

Life is a growing process. The longer we live, the more experiences we have and the more developed we become in our necessary life skills. Learn from your mistakes and don't keep repeating them. Neither allow yourself to live in the past. His mercies are new every morning. Learn to enjoy them.

MEDITATION 3

OVERCOMING TEMPTATION (A BATTLE OF THE MIND)

Now that we understand the importance of making good decisions, let's turn our attention to one of the specific battles we all face on a daily basis: the battle with temptation.

In Romans 7, Paul wrote about this ongoing, never-ending battle. As long as we are on Earth in these earthly bodies, we must fight the battle between the flesh and the spirit. No one is exempt. If you are determined to live for God, Satan and his cohorts will fight you every step of the way. But be encouraged. Jesus has already won the battle for us! He has equipped and empowered each of us to be overcomers, living a life of victory in this present world and the world to come.

To experience this victory on a daily basis, we must learn to walk in the Spirit and utilize the weapons of warfare at our disposal. The battle of every temptation always centers in the mind. Note what the Apostle James wrote concerning tempta-tion:

> From whence comes wars and fightings among you? Come they not hence, even of your lusts that war in your members? Ye lust, and have not: ye kill and desire to have, and cannot obtain: ye fight and war, yet ye have not, because ye ask not. Ye ask and receive not, because ye ask amiss, that ye may consume it upon your lusts. . . . Submit yourselves therefore to God. Resist the devil, and he will flee from you. Draw nigh to God, and He will draw nigh to you. Cleanse your hands, ye sinners; and purify your hearts, ye double minded. (James 4: 1–3; 7–8)

Only by the Holy Spirit's indwelling can we conquer and control the appetites of the flesh. There are three important facts we must know in order to be overcomers in this specific battle.

1. THE SOURCE OF TEMPTATION

Temptation does not come from God, but from our enemy. It grows more intense from our own desires and lust.

In His teaching on discipleship, Jesus emphasized the need for us to take up our cross and follow him. In this process, we must crucify the flesh and all of its desires. Paul testified to the Galatian church,

> I am crucified with Christ: nevertheless I live; yet not I, but Christ liveth in me: and the life which I now live in the flesh I live by the faith of the Son of God, who loved me, and gave Himself for me. (Galatians 2:20)

This is the secret to living in victory and overcoming temptation. We must daily come to the cross and submit every part of our being to the Lordship of Jesus Christ.

It is also important to know that temptation itself is not a sin. Jesus was tempted, yet the Bible clearly states that He lived a sinless life. Sin comes when we surrender to temptation rather than God in our daily walk.

2. LIFESTYLE PLAYS A ROLE

Even though the source of temptation is always Satan, we make it more difficult on ourselves by our lifestyles. This is what James was referencing when he said we are drawn away by our own lust.

We cannot take a casual approach to sin and expect to live in victory. We must be intentional in the music we listen to, the places of entertainment we visit, and the people we associate with.

In Romans 12:9, Paul exhorts us to "Let love be without dissimulation (false pretense; hiding our true character). Abhor that which is evil; cleave to that which is good." In our quest to become and remain overcomers, it is essential that we decide how we will live day by day. Living ethically with godly character is a matter of choice and discipline as previously discussed. Remind yourself often what Jesus taught: We are in this world but not of it. Our purpose is to be a living witness of God's saving grace.

Too many of God's family get distracted by the things available to us in this world's system and live their lives following pleasure rather than purpose. Unfortunately, they fail to understand that true happiness and joy comes only from following Christ and the purpose for which they were born. Again, to overcome temptation, we must daily partner with the Holy Spirit by acknowledging temptation's source.

3. TEMPTATION DOES NOT PLATEAU

We must understand the nature of temptation and its growth process in our lives. James puts this in perspective in his epistle to the Church:

> *Blessed is the man that endureth temptation: for when he is tried, he shall receive the crown of life, which the Lord hath promised to them that love Him. Let no man say when he is tempted, I am tempted of God: for God cannot be tempted with evil, neither tempteth he any man. But every man is tempted, when he is drawn away of his own lust, and enticed. Then when lust has conceived, it bringeth forth sin: and sin, when it is finished, bringeth forth death. (James 1:12–15)*

By feeding the desires of our flesh and exposing ourselves to the ungodly pleasures of this world, we birth a process that will always end in defeat and total destruction.

It is an ongoing battle. The only way we can win is to learn how to walk in the Spirit on a daily basis. Every day must begin at the cross, where we submit ourselves wholly to the lordship of Jesus Christ. It's not easy, but it is possible through the grace and love of God who gave us His son to die that we might live in victory.

Temptation is always centered on our carnal nature, and the enemy is wise in making it look attractive. If we keep our focus on Jesus, He will empower us with His Spirit to overcome all Satan's tricks, which aim to distract and deter us from God's purpose in our lives. Remember, the Word of God is the sword of the Spirit. We must use it to defeat the tempter, as Jesus did when tempted in the wilderness.

I urge you to prioritize Bible study. Saturate your hearts and minds with it on a daily basis. I personally believe this is what Jesus meant when He said, "Man shall not live by bread alone." As we feed on the Word of God, we mature and grow strong in our faith. It equips us to stand against the wiles of the devil and leads us into victorious living. Like the psalmist, we must learn the value of hiding God's word in our hearts that we might not sin against our God.

In summary, let me state again, the battle of temptation is real. But take heart, because it is winnable. Reread Paul's letter to the Romans and remind yourself who you are in Christ Jesus.

"What shall we then say to these things? If God be for us, who can be against us? Nay, in all these things we are more than conquerors through him that loved us." (Romans 8:31, 37)

I declare by the Word of God through the power of the Holy Spirit that we are victors, not victims.

MEDITATION 4
OVERCOMING WORRY, ANXIETY, AND FEAR

Be careful for nothing; but in everything by prayer and supplication with thanksgiving let your request be made known unto God. And the peace of God, which passeth all understanding, shall keep your hearts and minds through Christ Jesus.—Philippians 4:6–7

We live in a world shattered by chaos, confusion, and fear. The crises that we face are prophesied in God's Word, where we are taught the importance of keeping our eyes on Jesus.

And there shall be signs in the sun, and in the moon, and in the stars; and upon the earth distress of nations, with perplexity; the sea and the waves roaring; men's hearts failing them for fear, and for looking after those things which are coming on the earth: for the powers of heaven shall be shaken. And then shall they see the Son of Man coming in a cloud with power and great glory. And when these things begin to come to pass, then look up, and lift up your heads; for your redemption draweth nigh. (Luke 21:25–28)

There is no doubt in my mind that we are living in the last days of life on earth as we know it. If we focus on the conditions and problems we face on a daily basis, we will be overtaken by fear. Both worry and anxiety are birthed in fear.

In his writing to Timothy, Paul identifies fear as a "spirit." "For God hath not given us the spirit of fear; but of power, and of love, and of a sound mind." (2 Timothy 1:7) We must understand what we are fighting if we hope to overcome their influence in our lives. In our opening verses (Philippians 4:6–7), Paul teaches us how to deal with these enemies.

Over my years in pastoral ministry, I have seen many of God's precious people overcome by these formidable spirits. There are medications that can help, but the only way to conquer an evil spirit is through the power of the Holy Spirit.

Look closely at Paul's counsel. As believers in Jesus Christ, we should not allow ourselves to become anxious concerning the affairs of this life. He clearly states that we win these battles by utilizing two weapons given to us by our Heavenly Father.

1. PRAYER AND SUPPLICATION

The privilege and power of prayer are powerful weapons the enemy cannot withstand. Prayer brings us into the presence of God. No demon spirit can survive in that environment.

2. ATTITUDE OF GRATITUDE

Praise is powerful and will always drive these spirits out of our lives. Contrary to what many believers are taught, Satan cannot dwell in the presence of God for any length of time. When we turn our eyes upon Jesus and sincerely worship Him in spirit and truth, the enemy retreats.

Years ago, I went through a very dark valley that resulted in my being attacked over a period of several months. During that battle, I lost my vision of Christ and was buffeted by fear, worry, and horrible anxiety. Nights upon nights I wrestled with horrific spirits. As hard as I tried, I could neither sleep nor rest. The physical and spiritual effects were devastating.

After many weeks, I was led to Paul's counsel. In a weakened state of defeat, I began to walk around my prayer room, praising and worshiping God with all of my heart, while worship music played. Rather than focusing on my problem, I prayed in the Spirit, focusing on Jesus and His faithfulness to me. After about a week, I was falling asleep and sleeping all night without effort. I continue this practice today whenever I am troubled and having difficulty resting.

There is power in praise, and I have learned how to use it in battle. The precious privilege of prayer and praise has been given to us by our Heavenly Father to drive out worry, fear, and anxiety from our lives. When we develop a consistent prayer life enhanced by praise and worship, it gives God His proper place in our lives and puts the devil in his place.

It is not God's desire for us to be overcome by fear, worry, or anxiety. But in order for these principles to work effectively in our lives, there are some basic steps that we must take.

1. First and foremost, we should take a serious look at our relationship with God. Like David, we should daily invite the Holy Spirit to search our hearts and reveal anything that does not please Him. Any sinful attitude or activity will block God's peace and presence in our lives.

2. We must rid ourselves of selfishness and pride, understanding that both rob us of God's favor. We should stay close to the cross and allow the Holy Spirit to cleanse us of these barriers to God's blessings.

Scripture teaches us that if we abide in Him, our prayers will be effective and we will reap fruitful blessings. "If ye abide in Me, and my words abide in you, ye shall ask what ye will, and it shall be done unto you." (John 15:7)

Jesus also taught the importance of humility in our relationship with Him and others. In Luke 18, He teaches the parable of the Pharisee and the publican. Note His concluding thought:

> *"I tell you this man (the publican) went down to his house justified rather than the other; for everyone that exalteth himself shall be abased and he that (humbleth himself) shall be exalted." (Luke 18:14)*

Pride will never receive anything from our Heavenly Father, while humility will always bring victory.

3. We must be intentional in cultivating and maintaining an intimate relationship with Jesus. This is done simply through prayer, Bible reading, and worship. Each believer desperately needs to get involved in a local, Spirit-filled, Bible-believing church that will encourage and strengthen our faith through service and fellowship.

Victory over devastating spirits does not come automatically. We must fix our focus and continually keep our eyes upon Jesus, the author and finisher of our faith.

As we close this meditation, let me state again that our Heavenly Father has provided through Jesus Christ everything we need to live in peace and victory. Fear, worry, and anxiety are spiritual enemies that can be defeated if we maintain our focus and always seek to live in His Word.

MEDITATION 5
OVERCOMING TOXIC RELATIONSHIPS

The final area we will consider regarding how to live an overcoming life is to think seriously about the people you associate with on a regular basis. Our pastor teaches a principle in life that we should adopt: "Show me your friends, and I'll show you your future."

We become like those we hang out with. The wholeness of life is determined by our relationships. Pause for a few moments and reflect upon your life up to this moment. You are where you are and who you are courtesy of the powerful influence of the people you associate with.

Understanding this should motivate us to take a serious inventory of our lives—specifically who we have become and who influences us the most.

The importance of relationship is an intricate theme woven throughout the Old and New Testaments. We have been created in the image of God as tripartite beings (body, spirit, and soul). As such we have been created with a need to love and be loved. Therefore, it is totally understandable that we spend a lot of time, energy, and finances searching for meaningful relationships to fulfill this basic need.

With this in mind, we must embrace the truth that God has revealed Himself to us as our Heavenly Father. Through the sacrifice of Jesus Christ, we are adopted into His family, and the concept of relationship is found on every page of the Bible, His Word. God called Abraham a friend, and His deepest desire is to have a personal, intimate relationship with each one of us. He made this possible by sacrificing His only son on the cross, providing the possibility of knowing Him even as He knows us.

The tragedy of our generation is that thousands attend church every Sunday, worshiping God that they don't know. But Jesus did not come to start a religion. He was sent to reveal the Father to us so that we could have a personal relationship with Him.

> *In the beginning was the Word and the Word was with God, and the Word was God. And the Word was made flesh and dwelt among us, (and we beheld His glory, the glory as of the only begotten of the Father), full of grace and truth. (John 1:1, 14)*

Ultimately, our earthly relationships are determined by our relationship with God or the lack thereof. Our relationship with God can be greatly influenced, even altered, by our earthly relationships. Therefore, if we are to cultivate good and lasting relationships, we need to see the whole picture and cultivate relationships based on biblical teachings that confirm our creation as tripartite beings.

Positive relationships don't just happen. They must be created and cultivated intentionally by each person involved.

We all need family and friends for physical and emotional support in our lives. But only God can meet our spiritual needs. He has already done that by the way of the cross. However, it is our decision whether or not to enter into a close, intimate relationship with Him by accepting Christ into our hearts and committing to live according to His Word.

Earthly relationships will not function properly without a firm spiritual foundation. All relationships thrive or die based on the presence of the Holy Spirit in our lives.

With this in mind, let's now turn our thoughts on how to practically develop good, godly, lasting relationships.

We begin at creation, where we see what God intended for us in creating us after His image as tripartite beings. He gave us a body (physical), a spirit (emotional), and a soul (spiritual), As part of His plan, human beings experience relationships in the following three dimensions:

- Man/woman with God = spiritual intelligence/relationships
- Man/woman with self = emotional intelligence/relationships
- Man/woman with other man/woman = physical intelligence/relationships

In His creative wisdom, God created a natural flow of development that determines the success of all relationships. Foundationally, we come to know God as our Heavenly Father. We then develop a good relationship with ourselves. This is what Jesus referred to when He said we are to love others as we love ourselves. Thirdly, we cultivate relationships with others.

FIGHTING THE GOOD FIGHT

I've come to believe that when this natural flow is disrupted, we become confused and our relationships fail. I don't believe a person can come to know him or herself without knowing the God who created them.

In the same respect, how can we know and love someone else if we do not love ourselves in a pure way? This is clearly taught in the Old Testament (Leviticus 19:18) and by Jesus in the New Testament (Matthew 5:43). In creation, our Father created a spiritual principle that is reinforced in psychology today: We cannot love others until we learn how to properly love ourselves. The only way to achieve this is to see ourselves as God sees us and come to an understanding of His grace and love for us. Accepting this creates a sincere desire to know God and to love Him as He loves us. The natural outflowing of this is that we instinctively love ourselves and others as He loves us. The only way this happens is through the personal, inward working of the Holy Spirit in my life.

"And hope maketh not ashamed; because the love (of) God is shed abroad in our hearts by the Holy Ghost which is given unto us." (Romans 5:5) When I submit myself to the lordship of Jesus Christ in my life, His Spirit channels that natural flow and creates strong, lasting relationships with Him and others. Leave Him out of the equation, and our relationships become dysfunctional, dissatisfying, and in the end, destructive.

It is interesting to note that in the Bible, God uses three words to define love. Each of these words speaks to our tripartite personhood. They help us understand the natural flow of intimacy as God planned it.

- Agape = divine love
- Phileo = emotional love/friendships
- Eros = physical love/sexual expression

I define intimacy as a warm friendship marked by sincere love between friends and family. When developed in the above flow, our relationships are godly, good, and lasting. It is important that we take steps within this natural development to create meaningful relationships.

At this point, I suggest that we park for a few moments and honestly ask ourselves some revealing questions.

Why do so many of our relationships fail?

Why is divorce (even in the Church) at an all-time high, contributing to the demise of the family and the ultimate destruction of our nation?

How many lives have been scarred and destroyed by relationships that began in a fire of passion, only to diminish into hatred and uncontrollable anger, resulting in physical and emotional dysfunction?

As a pastor, I have been confronted with these realities more times than I want to remember. As a chaplain with our local police department and in a correctional facility, I have witnessed this heartbreaking scenario that destroys and scars people for life. The blunt truth is that what we are doing in our culture is not working. Our relationships fail us because we choose our way rather than God's. I have pondered this a lot. Through prayer, I believe the Holy Spirit has given me insight into this dilemma. Although it may be painful, let's consider the truth.

Here is a common scenario: We meet someone of interest and immediately begin a relationship on the intellectual level. It's nothing deep, but we share thoughts and feelings. If the relationship develops, we connect emotionally. Here is where we mess up. Without allowing the emotional relationship to fully develop, we immediately jump into a physical or sexual union, totally ignoring the spiritual.

FIGHTING THE GOOD FIGHT

The bedroom is hot and heavy. At first, we think we've found our Prince Charming or Miss America. Our life has finally produced a Cinderella story, and we can live happily ever after. But one day, we wake up and notice our Prince Charming or Miss America has become a frog. She no longer has the appeal she had in the beginning, and things in the bedroom aren't that exciting anymore. We focus on things that we don't like and become increasingly frustrated. Eventually, the whole thing explodes, leaving us disappointed and devastated.

What happened? Why didn't it work? This relationship failed because we ignored God's natural development of intimacy and did it our way instead of His. Every meaningful relationship must begin on the spiritual level. First, I must examine my own heart and be certain to put God first in everything. This is the only foundation that will survive life's challenges. Next, I need to make certain that the individual I'm pursuing also has a strong relationship with Jesus. Not just the Church, but a fervent love for God. If we don't share the same faith, there will always be something missing. A good foundation is essential if the house will survive life's storms.

I'm not talking about casual relationships. I have many relationships in the community where I live, through the businesses I use and the social activities I engage in. But I'm focusing on friendships and intimate relationships that chart the course of my life.

One of the most destructive lies Satan ever produced is the concept of "casual" sex. There is no such thing. God planned sex for our good and pleasure. When we defile it, sex loses its intended purpose. For a loving, sexual relationship to thrive, it must be birthed out of a spiritual and emotional relationship. That is God's way and the only way that it will survive.

Look back and examine your life, and you will discover it to be true. Sex is not a dirty word. God created us with sexual desires, and we can only experience the fullness of what He intended when we live within the context of His plan. We have become masters at destroying what God intended for good. If you really want to experience the optimum and have the best, try it His way. You will be amazed at the difference.

To fully comprehend this, we must take a closer look at the three expressions of love defined in Scripture and how each relates to the development of intimacy within the three dimensions of relationship.

During the development of the early Church, Scripture was written in Arabic Greek language. Greek is a very specific, pictorial language that conveys only one meaning for each word used. Unlike the English language, words never had dual meanings. The word love can be found in every book of the Bible, but it is used in three (tripartite) individual contexts. Understanding these specific meanings helps us have a better understanding of the three levels of love we experience in life.

Note again the three biblical words and their usage:

- **Agape** = Used exclusively to refer to God's love (spiritual and sacrificial)
- **Phileo** = Used to define love expressed to family and friends (affectionate and emotional)
- **Eros** = Used to define physical love (sensual and sexual)

In the English language, one word describes all three. The confusion is not only language-based. It is rooted more in our basic understanding of the concept of love and the level upon which we cultivate relationships. We need clarification on the specific meaning of each level of love and how to cultivate each level based on feelings and perceptions learned in life.

FIGHTING THE GOOD FIGHT

AGAPE

Agape love can only be experienced and expressed through spiritual revelation that only comes from God. "But God hath revealed them unto us by His Spirit: for the Spirit searcheth all things, yea, the deep things of God." (I Corinthians 2:10) We experience the wonderful love (agape) of God by revelation of the Holy Spirit, who leads us into the born-again experience. When we have truly been born again, He comes to live in us, thus enabling us to love Him, ourselves, and others with the same love He has toward us. "Now hope does not disappoint, because the love (of) God has been poured out in our hearts by the Holy Spirit who was given to us." (Romans 5:5)

Agape is selfless and sacrificial in nature. It can only be experienced and expressed through a personal relationship with our Lord Jesus Christ. It is spiritual and can only be understood in spiritual experience. This is why I firmly believe that if our emotional (phileo) and physical (eros) relationships are to survive and remain meaningful, they must be built upon the spiritual foundation of agape love.

In our culture, love is defined in terms of give and take. If you love me, I will love you. If you meet my needs, I will try to meet yours. In the minds of most, it is a contract rather than a covenant as God intended.

God's love is not only a paradox to our way of thinking, but also totally different from the world's view. Agape love is totally unconditional and always seeks ways to give rather than to receive. As we grow in our understanding of this kind of love by cultivating an intimate and personal relationship with Jesus, it opens our hearts and aids us in expressing this level of love for each other. Only then can we build all our relationships as Father intended.

PHILEO

Phileo is best understood within our modern culture as friendship. The actual meaning in Greek is "brotherly love," and is the word from which we get Philadelphia. It is the expression of love upon which family relationships and friendships are built. It is affectionate in nature and covers a myriad of needs in our lives. It is not as deep and intense as agape love but always sincere in expression.

I personally believe that true, biblical marriage must be experienced on the level of agape love where two (man and woman) become one through the miracle of God's love operating in us. This is the hunger of every human heart and the greatest need of our lives.

However, we have been created with a need for phileo also. We need good and positive relationships that extend beyond the covenant relationship of marriage. This is the kind of love shared between parents and children and brothers and sisters and is common in true friendships.

You might notice that when talking about friendships, I refer to "true" friends. Unfortunately, one of the painful lessons I have learned these many years in ministry is that in life we assimilate many relationships but very few friendships. The Bible teaches that a true friend will love you at all times, the good and the bad. "A man that hath friends must shew himself friendly: and there is a friend that sticketh closer than a brother." (Proverbs 18:24)

Most of us have had our hearts broken and our spirits deeply wounded due to fractured friendships. Betrayal creates a deep wound that only God can heal. One reason we have these painful experiences is that we develop friendships based on cultural understanding rather than principles taught in God's Word.

Fighting the Good Fight

We have been educated to believe that love is something we fall into and out of. It is totally based on feelings and differs from the love taught in Scripture. God's love is constant, even the phileo love expressed through friendships.

Because of the complexity of human nature, we all face challenges in our relationships with family and friends. If we build our relationships only on mutual affection, those relationships will not survive the crises we face. However, if we allow the Holy Spirit to change how we think, we can change the way we feel, thus building our relationships on God's kind of love.

Eros

The third and most popular kind of love in our sex-crazed society is the biblical expression of eros, which is sensual and sexual. Interestingly, it has the same meaning in Scripture, but without our cultural interpretation and stigma.

God's love is always pure and should only be experienced as He intended—in the context of marriage. In the sixties, we sought social change and freedom of sexual expression. Terms such as "free love" and "casual sex" became popular as our sense of morality decreased. "If it feels good," goes the saying, "then it must be okay."

Those in favor of "free love" achieved their goals. Now the very freedom they sought has created a prison of addiction, perversion, and lust that has eroded the stability of our nation, turning us into a sex-crazed people that has destroyed the sanctity of marriage and shattered the family unit upon which this great nation was built. Now without conscience, we offer innocent unborn children on the altar of sexual pleasure and idolatry through legalized abortion.

Sexual love was created and designed by God for pleasure

between a man and his wife. It is a beautiful gift that we have defiled through a spirit of perversion that threatens to destroy all that God intended for our good. When the physical relationship is placed before the spiritual, the much-needed emotional relationship is not permitted to develop naturally. The result will always be the same: the fire of passion will fizzle, infidelity will sneak in, trust will be destroyed, hearts will be broken, and homes will fall apart, leaving children and all involved in the ashes of despair and dysfunction. This is always the fruit of worshiping at the altar of pleasure.

How long will we continue down this destructive path, always getting what we have always gotten? What will it take for us to wake up and admit that change is not only possible but necessary?

Before we close this meditation, pause for a time of prayer and reflection. Ask if any anger and bitterness in your heart was planted in your spirit through broken and failed relationships. Is it conceivable that others have a hard time loving you because you don't love yourself properly?

When we experience failure in life, it damages our self-esteem and how we view ourselves. But I have good news (Gospel). Jesus is our Healer.

And there was delivered unto him the book of the prophet Esaias. And when he had opened the book, he found the place where it was written, the Spirit of the Lord is upon me, because He hath anointed me to preach the Gospel to the poor; He hath sent me to heal the (brokenhearted), to preach deliverance to the captives, and recovering of sight to the blind, to set at liberty them that are (bruised), to preach the acceptable year of the Lord. (Luke 4:17–19)

FIGHTING THE GOOD FIGHT

Yes, it is possible for you to change. But only through the grace and love of God.

I know that this has been a very intense meditation. I encourage you to plant it in your heart and embrace the pain. Don't resist it. Pain is a great motivator for change. As God heals your wounds, He will renew your mind and help you prevent your past from destroying your future.

As we close our focus on this all topic of relationships, let me share four simple, powerful steps to ensure our relationships are godly, good, and lasting.

STEP 1: BUILD A FOUNDATION OF TRUST

Whether in marriage, family, or friendship, a relationship can only thrive when built on a foundation of trust. Trust is defined as "being faithful at all times and in every situation." No relationship can survive without it.

Trust does not come easily. It is birthed out of commitment and comes only as we prove ourselves worthy of its virtue. It is developed through difficult times and is matured in the complexity of crises we face. Just as fire purifies, the trials we face are a proving ground to develop genuine trust in our character.

Note the counsel of James to the early Church in his epistle.

> *My brethren, count it all joy when ye fall into divers temptations; knowing this, that the trying of your faith worketh patience. But let patience have her perfect work, that ye may be perfect and entire, wanting nothing. (James 1:2–4)*

Trust is an indicator of who we really are. If we cave under pressure, lie to protect ourselves, cut corners, cheat, and manipulate others to our advantage, they will soon learn that we are not trustworthy. However, if we practice honesty and humility, acknowledging our mistakes even if it hurts, and always honor our word, the influence of our character will prove that we can be trusted.

STEP 2: ESTABLISH RESPECT

Every relationship must display sincere respect to survive. Respect grows out of our affection and honor of others. It is commonly expressed in attitude and activity.

When we respect someone, we sincerely speak terms of endearment and consider it an honor to serve them by putting their needs before our own.

Like trust, respect is earned. It is conveyed through position and living a consistent lifestyle that is always favoring others ahead of ourselves. If we respect others, they will find it easy to respect us. If a relationship is to thrive, each person involved must value the other and live a life worthy of their respect.

STEP 3: MAINTAIN MUTUALITY

The third step is the glue necessary to stabilize all relationships. That step is developing and maintaining a sense of mutuality. By mutuality I mean shared, reciprocal affection and respect between those involved. Simply put, both parties like each other and enjoy fellowship on the same level.

Love, by its nature, demands a response and will fade in the absence of one. Although agape is unconditional, human relationships require a common interest. One of the most important lessons I've learned in fifty-three years of ministry is that a true friendship cannot be forced. Like many, I have been deeply hurt and suffered a damaged self-esteem due to the rejection of someone I desired a friendship with who did not share the same desire.

Regardless of painful experiences, we must maintain open hearts and minds and discipline ourselves not to be governed by past failures. Mutuality is not something we can force on anyone, but it can be nurtured through self-control and maintaining a right spirit.

STEP 4: COMMUNICATE CONSTANTLY

The final step to enhance relationships is to develop the ability to communicate. Learning to communicate effectively is essential for strong relationships.

Communication is defined as "the clear exchange of ideas, information, and feelings between two or more individuals."

Most of us assume when we talk, others hear and understand what we are saying. This is not always true. Talking alone does not constitute communication. Listening is a major component of clear communication. Listening is intentional and must be learned in order to be effective communicators. I must understand that everything I hear gets filtered through my emotions and experiences.

Let me illustrate this with a personal experience.

As part of my pastoral ministry, I had the privilege to serve my community as a certified police chaplain. I attended the Police Academy so I could qualify to ride along with officers in the field during their shifts. This enabled me to experience first hand what these men and women encounter on a daily basis. It also gave me a deep respect and love for these selfless individuals. Over the years I have been greatly blessed with many friends through this ministry.

On one Friday afternoon, I took a ride-along with the shift supervisor. We were called to a dangerous scene where a young African-American man with mental issues brandished a forty-five-caliber pistol. He shot cars, houses, and anything else in sight. The entire neighborhood was shut down.

Upon arrival, we attempted to establish communication with the young man who threatened to kill himself. The more we talked, the more agitated he became. It was clear that we were not reaching him. We positioned ourselves safely behind the police cruiser and continued trying to communicate with him with no success.

It was apparent to me that the young man and the officers on scene were in grave danger. I paused and prayed, asking for wisdom to help this troubled man. The Holy Spirit quietly spoke to my heart to look around and note the officers on site. As a coincidence, all the officers were white. The young man kept yelling the same thing repeatedly: "They are going to kill me!"

I suddenly saw the situation from his perspective and suggested to the supervisor that we call in a black officer. He agreed. Shortly, a black female officer arrived. In a few moments, she established communication with the young man. Subsequently, he surrendered to her custody with no one getting injured.

In follow-up, we found that the young man had long suffered from debilitating mental illness. That morning, he received a new medication and was having a bad reaction. To make matters worse, he had been raised in a family that taught that police officers were the enemy and they should be killed on sight. This young man was processing the situation through the lens he had been taught. Fortunately, with God's help, serious injury and death were avoided and the situation ended peacefully, with the young man getting the help he needed.

Not all situations are this dramatic, but we must be observant and listen carefully when attempting to communicate with others. Communication is an acquired life skill that we need to employ in order to maintain good relationships.

A concluding thought for prayerful meditation. Intimate personal relationships with family and friends are basic needs. Good relationships don't just happen. They must be nurtured with an understanding of the three dimensions designed by our Heavenly Father. We must pursue the natural development of intimacy as planned and intended by God, our Creator. By going God's way instead of our way, we experience life with the happiness and fulfillment we both need and God desires for us.

ADDENDUM

Before you close this book, let me encourage you to take a few days to prayerfully reflect on what you have gained in this experience. Knowledge is wonderful, but it is of no value unless you apply it to your life. "But be doers of the Word and not hearers only, deceiving your own selves." (James 1:22)

Ask your Heavenly Father to search your heart and to give you the courage to acknowledge what needs changing in your life. Then pursue that change with all your heart.

It is my sincere prayer that the time you have given to share these meditations will provide a life-changing experience.

Submit yourselves therefore to God. Resist the devil, and he will flee from you. Draw nigh to God, and He will draw nigh to you. Cleanse your hands, ye sinners; and purify your hearts, ye double minded. (James 4:7–8)

—Pastor Larry Briggs